Celebrating Buddhist FESTIVALS

NICK HUNTER

raintree

3 8002 02318 847 9

Raintree is an imprint of Capstone Global Library Limited, a company incorporated in England and Wales having its registered office at 7 Pilgrim Street, London, EC4V 6LB – Registered company number: 6695582

www.raintree.co.uk
myorders@raintree.co.uk

Text © Capstone Global Library Limited 2016
The moral rights of the proprietor have been asserted.

Edited by James Benefield
Designed by Steve Mead
Original illustrations © Capstone Global Library Limited
Illustrated by HL Studios
Picture research by Eric Gohl
Production by Helen McCreath
Originated by Capstone Global Library Limited
Printed and bound in China

ISBN 978 1 406 29771 3 (hardback)
19 18 17 16 15
10 9 8 7 6 5 4 3 2 1

ISBN 978 1 406 29778 2 (paperback)
20 19 18 17 16
10 9 8 7 6 5 4 3 2 1

British Library Cataloguing in Publication Data
A full catalogue record for this book is available from the British Library.

Acknowledgements
Alamy: Art Directors & TRIP, 43, Darby Sawchuk, 9, Hemis, 42, Robert Harding Picture Library Ltd, 38; AP Photo: Wong Maye-E, cover; BigStockPhoto.com: shanin, 26; Capstone Studio: Karon Dubke, 14–15 (all), 24¬–25 (all), 30–31 (all); Corbis: Demotix/Maji, 34, Keren Su, 28; Dreamstime: Kongsky, 10, Misuhashistock, 39; Getty Images: AFP/Orlando Kissner, 23; Newscom: EPA/Rungroj Yongrit, 17, Eye Ubiquitous, 22, FeatureChina/Nava Chung, 40, Picture Alliance/Godong/Philippe Lissac, 21, Picture Alliance/Godong/Robert Mulder, 29, Polaris/Dario Pignatelli, 37, Reuters/Kin Cheung, 35, UIG Universal Images Group/Godong, 32, Visual & Written, 41, Xinhua News Agency/Chogo, 13, Xinhua News Agency/Purbu Zhaxi, 12, ZUMA Press/Ben Cawthra, 11, ZUMA Press/Ian Buswell, 8; Shutterstock: beebrain, 19, Calvin Chan, 20, Daimond Shutter, 4, Dietmar Temps, 7, Hong Vo, 46, PeoGeo, 33; SuperStock: Steve Vidler, 18.

Design Elements: Shutterstock

We would like to thank Peggy Morgan for her invaluable help in the preparation of this book.

Every effort has been made to contact copyright holders of material reproduced in this book. Any omissions will be rectified in subsequent printings if notice is given to the publisher.

SAFETY TIPS FOR THE RECIPES
Trying new recipes is fun, but before you start working in the kitchen, keep these safety tips in mind:
- Always ask an adult for permission, especially when using the hob, oven or sharp knives.
- At the hob, always point saucepan handles away from the edge. Don't keep flammable materials, such as towels, too close to the burners. Have a fire extinguisher nearby. Don't lean too close when you lift a lid off a pan – steam can cause burns, too. Always use oven gloves when taking dishes out of the oven.
- Wash your hands before you work, and wash your workspace and utensils after you are done. Cook foods completely. Don't use expired or spoiled food. Be careful when you cut with knives.
- Work with an adult – together you can both learn about religions of the world through food!

CONTENTS

Some words are shown in bold, **like this**. You can find out what they mean by looking in the glossary.

INTRODUCING BUDDHISM

Buddhism is a religion followed by more than 375 million people around the world. Unlike many other religions, it is not based on the belief in a god or gods. Buddhists follow the life and teachings of the Buddha. Buddhists try to develop their hearts and minds to achieve a deeper understanding of life.

⋀ There are many statues of the Buddha, which usually show him in a state of meditation.

Buddhist teachings

The teachings of the Buddha spread out from India in the centuries after his death. Followers understood his teaching in different ways, leading to different branches of Buddhism. The two main groups are **Theravada** Buddhism and **Mahayana** Buddhism. In general, Theravada Buddhists follow the words and teachings of the Buddha most closely. The Mahayana tradition places most emphasis on a person's path to **enlightenment**. Although most Buddhists live in Asia, the religion has now spread to many other parts of the world.

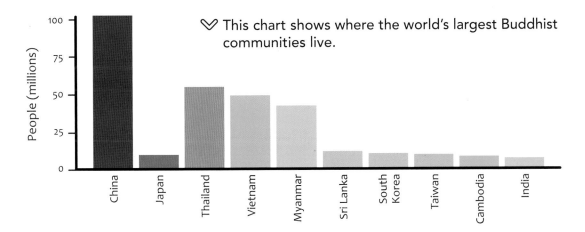

This chart shows where the world's largest Buddhist communities live.

Buddhism in Britain

The first Buddhist societies in Britain were set up in the early 1900s. Britain's Buddhist population was very small until the 1950s, when many people started to move to the country from Asia. There are now more than 250,000 Buddhists in Britain.

The Buddha

Siddhartha Gautama was born into a rich Indian family more than 2,500 years ago. He lived a **privileged** life until he chose to leave his palace and came across people in real **poverty** and suffering. Siddhartha then led a life without luxury but also without hardship, for example extreme poverty. Buddhists believe that, when Siddhartha was meditating, he gained a deeper understanding of life and became enlightened. He was then known as the Buddha, or the "enlightened one".

Buddhist festivals

Buddhist communities celebrate many special days and festivals throughout the year. Some festivals, such as Vesak or Buddha Day, are celebrated by all Buddhists, although the dates and traditions of the festivals vary.

Different kinds of festivals

The **monastic sangha**, the community of **monks** and, in some cases, **nuns**, is very important in many types of Buddhism. Uposatha Days are special days every month. On these days, ordinary Buddhists spend time at **monasteries**. Some of these Uposatha days are celebrated as festivals, such as Vesak.

Mahayana Buddhists do not take part in Uposatha days. However, they do celebrate a range of festivals connected to the Buddha's life.

The Buddha's teachings

The Buddha taught that life was a cycle of birth, death and rebirth. All life involves change, which makes it seem unsatisfactory. This causes suffering, and the release from suffering comes from following the Noble Eightfold Path. To follow this path, Buddhists should "walk" a middle way between too much luxury and hardship.

CALENDAR OF BUDDHIST FESTIVALS

Dates of festivals are calculated according to the Buddhist calendar, based on the movements of the Moon. As a result, dates vary slightly every year if you are looking at the Western, or Gregorian, calendar.

Month	Festival	Month	Festival
January	New Year (Mahayana)	July	Asalha Puja or Dharma Day (Theravada)
February	Parinirvana Day (Mahayana) Losar – Tibet (Mahayana)		Start of Vassa (Theravada) Esala Perahera – Sri Lanka (Theravada)
March	Magha Puja or Sangha Day – (Theravada)		
April	New Year (Theravada) Songkran – Thailand (Theravada) Hana Matsuri – Japan	August	Festival of Hungry Ghosts – China (Mahayana)
May	Vesak	October	Tavatimsa – Myanmar (Theravada)
June	Poson – Sri Lanka (Theravada)	November	Kathina (Theravada)

Food and festivals

Buddhists believe that it is important not to be greedy with food. Food is often offered to others, particularly to those living in monastries. Many Buddhists **fast**, or go without food, on special days during the year.

⌃ Buddhists offer food to monastics. For example, this can happen on Uposatha days.

BUDDHIST NEW YEAR

The New Year is a great time of celebration for most Buddhists. It combines Buddhist ideas about renewal and rebirth with traditions of each region or community. The New Year has different names in different communities, such as Songkran in Thailand and Losar in Tibet.

The New Year festival is a time of renewal. Buddhists clean statues of the Buddha and drape them with robes. People clean their houses from top to bottom.

Many New Year rituals involve water, including pouring it over the hands of monks and others as a sign of respect. People reflect on the past year and commit themselves to the Buddhist life.

⌃ Buddhists in Thailand clean a statue of the Buddha during the Songkran festival.

When is the New Year celebrated?

The time for marking the Buddhist New Year varies from the middle of January for many Mahayana communities to mid-April in Theravadin countries, such as Thailand and Sri Lanka. The festival normally lasts for up to four days.

Kindness to animals

Buddhists believe that the New Year is a time of forgiveness and helping others. They show this by releasing caged birds and being kind to all living things. Not harming living things is a basic belief for many Buddhists. Many, but not all, Buddhists are vegetarian.

⌃ When a Buddhist releases a caged bird, he or she gains great merit for his or herself.

Sand and water

Water is a key part of many New Year celebrations, especially in the Thai New Year festival of Songkran, which is celebrated for a week in April. The festival falls at the hottest time of the year, so during the celebrations people cool down by spraying each other with water.

There are many other ways of celebrating in Asia. In Thailand, Cambodia and Laos, Buddhists visit their temples or nearby riverbanks with small bags of sand on the day before the New Year. They shape the sand into the shape of small temples.

The next day, the sand is spread out over the temple floor or washed away by the river. This ritual symbolizes the cleansing of bad deeds from the year before.

⌃ Mounds of sand are built in the shape of stupas, or sacred domed buildings.

British Buddhists at New Year

Buddhist communities in countries outside Asia also celebrate New Year, but in slightly different ways. The Wat Buddhapadipa temple in Wimbledon, London, celebrates the Thai Songkran festival. Members of the community meet at the temple for religious activities and entertainment. New Year is a time for families and for remembering family members who have died. Visitors to the temple wash their faces in the morning and their feet in the evening as a sign of a fresh start.

» Kite-flying is a colourful feature of many Buddhist New Year festivals.

Karma

Buddhists believe that living things are reborn. The form this rebirth takes depends on their past acts and the law of **karma**. Different sins can lead to rebirth as an animal or a ghost. Acts of kindness, generosity or reaching a state of spiritual calm can lead to a good rebirth. Doing good deeds during festivals such as New Year can bring good karma.

⌃ Losar is a time for sacred rituals, but also for less formal celebration. These dancers are rehearsing a dance for a Losar TV show.

Losar

Tibet is a remote mountain country with its own special style of Buddhism. Tibetan Buddhism has lots of rituals and festivals. There is no more important festival here than Losar, the Tibetan New Year, which is celebrated for three days in February.

The first day of Losar is a time to celebrate with family. On the following two days, Tibetans visit their friends and neighbours. Tibetans also visit monasteries and give offerings to the monks and nuns. The start of the New Year is celebrated by sharing special kapse, a type of cake.

The Great Prayer Festival

The fourth day after the start of Losar is the start of Monlam Chenmo, or the Great Prayer Festival, which lasts for eight days. Taking part is seen as good for the karma of the individual and the whole community. Traditionally, monks would take exams at this time to gain higher qualifications. Tibetan Buddhists are reminded that nothing lasts forever by the melting of great sculptures made of butter, dyed in various colours. These are displayed in homes and monasteries during Losar.

Now & Then

Before Losar

In many religions, festivals have been adapted over time. Before Buddhism arrived in Tibet in the 7th century CE, Tibetans already enjoyed a mid-winter festival at this time of year. They made offerings of **incense** to local spirits. Driving out evil spirits is still part of the rituals around Losar.

The month after Losar is dedicated to driving out evil spirits from the previous year. On the 14th day of the month, monks dress in colourful costumes and masks to perform a sacred dance. The dance is accompanied by music played on instruments such as drums, horns and oboes.

▽ Monks wear masks, like these, to frighten off evil spirits.

Vegetarian
guthuk

Guthuk is a soup only eaten once a year on the evening before Losar. The soup contains dumplings with hidden fortune messages. The soup needs to have at least nine ingredients – number nine is good luck.

TIME:

About 1 hour

SERVES:

Makes 3-4 small servings

TOOLS:

weighing scales
knife and cutting board
large saucepan
stirring spoon
mixing bowl
baking sheet
fortune slips

- **V**egetarian
- **V**egan
- **D**airy Free

INGREDIENTS:

Soup:
½ tablespoon vegetable oil
½ a medium onion, finely chopped
½ teaspoon chopped garlic
½ teaspoon red pepper flakes
1 teaspoon chopped fresh ginger
stalk of celery, sliced
50 g leeks, white and light green parts, sliced
70 g cabbage, shredded
1 spring onion, chopped
½ tablespoon soy sauce
500 ml water
salt and pepper to taste

Dumplings and noodles:
125 g plain flour, plus a little more for dusting
¼ teaspoon salt
65 ml water

See page 44 for more cookery tips for this recipe

STEPS:

1 Heat the oil in the large saucepan on medium heat. Add the onion and sauté (fry) for about 5 minutes. Add the garlic and ginger. Sauté for about 2 minutes more.

2 Add the celery, leeks, cabbage, red pepper flakes, soy sauce, water, salt and pepper. Bring to a boil, cover and reduce heat. Simmer for about 30 minutes.

3 Meanwhile, mix the flour and salt in a bowl. Stir in the water a little at a time until you have a soft dough. Knead it about 10 times on a floured surface (see page 44 for kneading tips).

4 Pinch off four 3-cm balls of dough. Flatten each one, place a fortune slip in the middle, and reroll. Heat the water in a saucepan until boiling. Add the dumplings and cook until the dumplings rise to the top, for about 10 minutes.

5 Pinch off bits of the remaining dough, pressing them flat. Place these noodles on a floured baking sheet.

6 Add the noodles to the soup. Bring back to a boil and cook until they rise to the surface, for about 5 minutes.

7 Ladle the soup into bowls. Place a dumpling in the centre of each one. Sprinkle the spring onions on as a garnish. Ask guests to open their fortune dumplings and set them aside before they eat. You do not eat the fortune balls or messages!

MAGHA PUJA

The festival of Magha Puja commemorates an important event from the Buddha's life. This is when he preached to a crowd of 1,250 monks, who had gathered together without any planning. The Buddha preached to the crowd, urging them to do good and to help purify the world. This festival of lights takes place on the first full days of full moon in March.

Magha Puja is sometimes called the Fourfold Assembly Day, because four things united the monks who listened to the Buddha:

- They were all arhats, or monks who had completed the path to enlightenment
- The monks had all been **ordained** by the Buddha
- They had gathered by chance
- They met on the day of the full moon in March.

The festival is celebrated on that day in most Buddhist countries. Sangha Day is another name for Magha Puja. The sangha is the fourfold community of monks, nuns, Buddhist men and women.

Celebrating Magha Puja

On Magha Puja day, Buddhist communities will meet at their local temple, bringing food and gifts for the monks. The festival of lights is celebrated with the lighting of 1,250 candles representing the 1,250 monks who gathered to hear the Buddha speak. Candles are also carried in processions.

Three Precious Jewels

At Magha Puja and other festivals, Buddhists walk around a **shrine** or statue of the Buddha three times. This marks the Three Precious Jewels or Refuges of Buddhism: the Buddha, the **Dharma** (his teaching) and the Sangha (the fourfold community). The Buddha said that his followers could take refuge in and treasure these Jewels when following the Noble Eightfold Path to enlightenment.

⌃ Candles are lit in Buddhist temples during Magha Puja. In this dramatic picture, thousands of Thai Buddhist monks take part in a candle-lit procession to mark this festival.

VESAK

Vesak is the most important Buddhist festival of the year. Most Buddhists celebrate Vesak on the first days of full moon in May, or sometimes early June. Vesak is celebrated by Buddhists around the world. As with many Buddhist festivals, the meaning and traditions of the festival can vary from one country to another.

Buddha Day

For Theravada Buddhists, Vesak marks the birth, enlightenment and death of the Buddha. Mahayana Buddhists celebrate these three events at different times of the year. For these Buddhists, Vesak is the Buddha's birthday.

Birth, enlightenment and death

Buddhists believe that the Buddha's birth was accompanied by many miracles. He could walk and talk as soon as he was born and declared, "I am born for supreme knowledge, for the welfare of the world, thus this is my last birth."

≪ Buddhist temples are often decorated with scenes from the Buddha's life. In this one, he is shown beneath the Bodhi tree where he achieved enlightenment.

The Buddha's birth is celebrated by pouring water over statues of a baby Buddha. When he achieved enlightenment, the Buddha freed himself from the cycle of birth, death and rebirth.

According to Buddhist **scriptures**, the Buddha reached the final enlightenment (parinirvana) at his death, about 45 years after his enlightenment beneath the Bodhi tree. These are the events celebrated by many Buddhists at Vesak.

Teaching and learning

Vesak is a time for Buddhists to learn more about the teachings of the Buddha. They may listen to lectures at temples about the Buddha's life.

Vesak is a joyful time, with lots of **chanting** and praying. Visitors to a temple bring presents of food for the monastic community or leave gifts at the feet of the Buddha's statue.

≫ In this ceremony in Thailand, Buddhists give alms to more than 1,000 monastics at Vesak.

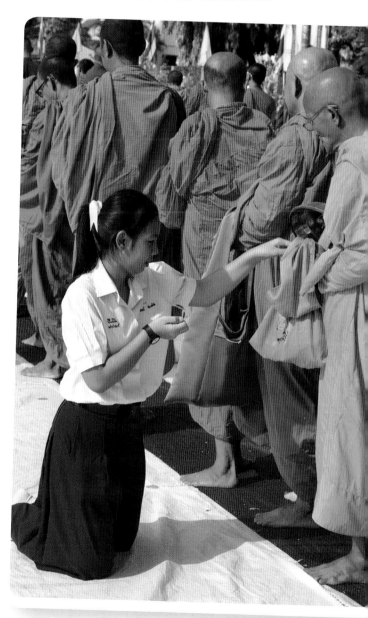

Celebrating Vesak

Buddhist communities around the world celebrate Vesak in different ways. In many countries, Vesak is a festival of light. Lanterns made from wood and paper are hung in houses from Sri Lanka to Thailand. Street processions are held in countries such as Malaysia.

Local traditions become part of the wider Buddhist festival. For example, in China, people take part in colourful dragon dances.

This elaborate float is part of a Vesak procession in Kuala Lumpur, Malaysia.

Respecting nature

In Myanmar, Bodhi trees are watered at the festival, to recognize that the Buddha gained enlightenment beneath this type of tree. Flowers are everywhere in Vesak decorations, reminding Buddhists about the changing nature of life.

Caring for nature and avoiding harm to living things are always important for Buddhists, but especially so at Vesak. Some farmers stop work during the festival, so they do not harm animals.

⌃ Buddhist families make a special effort to eat vegetarian food at Vesak.

Vesak in Britain

In countries where most of the population is Buddhist, Vesak is a festival that involves the whole country. However, the festival is just as important for Buddhists in countries where only a minority of people follow the religion.

For many British Buddhists, Vesak is focused on celebrations at temples and Buddhist community centres. These communities organize work and donations for charity.

Street parties

The people of Sri Lanka celebrate Vesak in several ways. For example, they stage plays and mime performances that recreate scenes from the Buddha's life. Elsewhere, illuminated and painted structures called Vesak pandals are set up showing scenes from the Buddha's life. Celebrating Buddhists are given free food and drink from stalls lining the streets.

HANA MATSURI

The ultimate flower-filled Buddhist festival is the Japanese celebration of Hana Matsuri, which means "floral festival". This celebration is also called Kanbutsue. It is the Japanese way of celebrating the Buddha's birthday.

Now & Then

Origins of Hana Matsuri

Before Buddhism came to their country, the Japanese already celebrated a flower festival in spring, when they gathered wild mountain flowers. The Japanese believed this ritual would protect the vital rice harvest.

⌃ The flowers of Hana Matsuri celebrate the coming of spring as well as the Buddha's birth.

On 8 April every year, Japanese Buddhists create beautiful gardens of paper flowers. These represent the gardens of Lumbini, where the Buddha was born. Small model buildings are created and covered with flowers. Inside each building is a small statue of the baby Buddha. The gardens may also contain white elephants made of papier mâché. This is a reminder of the story that the Buddha's mother dreamed of a rare white elephant before the Buddha's birth.

Perfumed water

During the festival, the statue is sprinkled with a type of tea called ama-cha. Some worshippers drink this tea as a form of holy water. This ritual is based on the tradition that the Buddha's first bath was in water that had been perfumed by the gods.

Japanese Buddhism

Buddhism spread to Japan from China and Korea around the 6th century CE. There are many different Buddhist movements within Japan. For example, some Japanese Buddhists follow aspects of the ancient Japanese Shinto religion. Elsewhere, followers of the form of Buddhism founded by the monk Nichiren do not celebrate traditional Japanese festivals. They have their own special days during the year.

▽ Local Buddhist traditions can often travel with believers as they move around the world. These Japanese people, now living in Brazil, are making an offering for Hana Matsuri.

Rice pudding

This rice pudding is sometimes known as kheer. It's a creamy mix of rice and milk, and is a popular treat during Vesak. It reminds Buddhists of the story of the maiden who offered a golden bowl of porridge to Buddha.

This is a very simple recipe to make, with only a handful of ingredients.

TIME:
About 45 minutes

SERVES:
4 people

TOOLS:
weighing scales
large saucepan
stirring spoon

Vegetarian

Gluten Free

INGREDIENTS:

700 ml whole milk
40 g white rice
40 g white granulated sugar
¼ teaspoon ground cardamom (you can grind these
        seeds yourself in a pestle and mortar)
60 g pistachios, chopped
¼ teaspoon almond extract

STEPS:

1 Bring the milk to a simmer over medium heat. Add the rice. Reduce the heat and simmer, uncovered, for about 30 minutes until the rice is soft and the amount of milk has been reduced by about half. Stir very frequently so that the milk and rice do not stick to the bottom of the pan.

Remove from the heat. Add the sugar, cardamom, pistachios and almond extract.

2

3 Sir the mixture in the pan well. You can serve this dish hot or cold.

Poson And Esala Perahera

Sri Lanka is home to more than 15 million Buddhists. The festival that celebrates the arrival of the first Buddhists more than 2,000 years ago is one of the highlights of the Sri Lankan year. People across the island celebrate the festival but the festivities are centred on two ancient places: the temple complex at Mihintale and the town of Anuradhapura.

At Mihintale, Mahinda is believed to have converted Sri Lanka's king to Buddhism. Mahinda was the son of the Indian Emperor Ashoka who, as a Buddhist, had also helped religion to spread during his own reign. When the full moon appears in June, thousands of Buddhists come and fill Mihintale's streets in honour of Mahinda.

Anuradhapura is where Mahinda's sister Sanghamitta is said to have planted a branch of the original Bodhi tree under which the Buddha achieved enlightenment. She also started the order of nuns there. She is honoured on the full moon day in December.

▽ Mihintale has become a centre for pilgrimage for Sri Lanka's Buddhists.

Parties and processions

For most Sri Lankans, Poson is a time for street parties and celebrations. Sri Lankans parade through the streets, carrying images of Mahinda, accompanied by musicians and drummers. Processions like this, which are part of many Sri Lankan festivals, are called perahera.

Now & Then

Buddhism comes to Sri Lanka

The Buddhist religion has been the main faith in Sri Lanka longer than in any other country in the world. The Buddha's teaching was introduced to the country by Mahinda and Venerable Sanghamitta in the 3rd century BCE. From Sri Lanka, Buddhism spread to countries such as Thailand via trade routes.

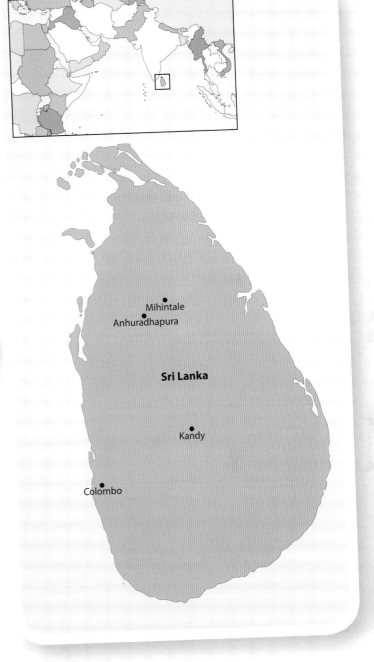

⌃ This map shows some of the most important sites for Sri Lankan Buddhists.

Festival of the tooth

Poson is closely followed by another Sri Lankan festival. The festival of Esala Perahera is the biggest event of the year in the city of Kandy. For 10 nights in July and August, the people of Kandy and thousands of visitors honour and celebrate an ancient **relic** believed to be a tooth from the Buddha himself.

⋁ Sri Lanka is the oldest continually Buddhist country. Its ancient shrines and sites are central to the country's festivals.

Now & Then

The origins of Esala Perahera

This unusual and fascinating festival began in the 4th century CE when the relic arrived in Sri Lanka. The country's ruler at the time ordered that the sacred tooth should be carried in a procession every year. During the island's long history, the tooth moved to different homes. Portuguese invaders even claimed they had destroyed it. Local people denied this and built a special temple to house this precious relic.

Esala Perahera begins with the ceremonial chopping up of a specially blessed jackfruit tree into four pieces. These pieces are then taken to shrines around the city.

For five nights, there are celebrations around these shrines. On the sixth night, processions start to move through the streets towards the Sri Dalada Maligawa (Temple of the Tooth), where the relic is kept. Each night, processions become more lavish and colourful.

The festical ends with a procession by more than 100 elephants wearing dazzling costumes. Alongside the elephants are drummers, musicians and dancers. The largest elephant carries the gold casket of the sacred tooth. The skies above Kandy are lit up by firework displays.

⌂ The streets of Kandy are full of people for the climax of Esala Perahera.

Potato
curry

During Poson, Sri Lankans set up stalls, called dansala, to serve free meals to others. People work together in the spirit of giving to serve rice and curry to thousands. Ala Hodi, a mix of potatoes, onions, coconut milk and spices is a favourite curry in Sri Lanka.

It is easy to double, or even triple, this recipe if you want to share it with a crowd. It is a good dish to bring family or friends together.

TIME:

About 30 minutes

SERVES:

4 people

See page 44 for more cookery tips for this recipe.

 Vegetarian

Gluten Free

TOOLS:

weighing scales
knife and cutting board
large saucepan
stirring spoon

INGREDIENTS:

3 medium white potatoes
1 small onion
1 or 2 deseeded green chillies (depending on how spicy you would like it!)
1 tablespoon curry powder
1 teaspoon salt
1 small cinnamon stick
500 ml unsweetened coconut milk (liquid and solids whisked together)

STEPS:

1 Peel and chop the potatoes into 2 cm x 2 cm cubes. Slice the small onion. Slice the chillies, remove the seeds and dice it.

2 Heat a large saucepan on medium and add all of the ingredients. Stir them all to combine.

Get the mixture simmering and keep it simmering. Cook uncovered for about 20 to 30 minutes, stirring frequently, until the mixture has thickened and the potatoes are soft when pierced with a fork.

3

4 Remove the cinnamon stick. Serve the curry with bread or with rice.

ASALHA PUJA AND VASSA

After achieving enlightenment, the Buddha spoke to five men who he knew were also on a spiritual quest in a deer park near Benares, India. In his speech, he explained what he had learned and how they could also reach enlightenment. This was the start of the Buddha's teaching.

The **sermon** at Benares is celebrated by Theravada Buddhists in the festival of Asalha Puja on the day of the full moon in July. This is a very important festival as it marks the time when the first Buddhists followed the Buddha's teaching.

⌄ This statue shows the Buddha preaching to his five followers at Benares.

The Rains

In India and many parts of Asia, July is the start of the rainy season. In the past, the heavy rains made it difficult to travel. So this became a time for people to stay in their monasteries and practise deep meditation.

Theravada Buddhists call the rainy season Vassa, which means "the Rains". It lasts for three months. During Vassa, ordinary Buddhists sometimes choose to live in a monastery and use the time to study and **meditate**.

Buddhists do not arrange family celebrations such as weddings at this time. Many Theravada Buddhists take care to mark Uposatha days during Vassa, taking gifts of food for the monks. In Britain, this **retreat** period is often marked between January and March.

Dharma Day

Asalha Puja is often called Dharma Day, particularly in Buddhist communities outside Asia. Dharma is the word used for the Buddha's teaching. It means "truth" or "law". This teaching began with the first sermon at Benares, which Buddhists sometimes call "the first turning of the wheel of law".

▽ The days leading up to Asalha Puja are a popular time for new monks and nuns to be ordained. Here, a mother is helping to ordain her son.

Mahayana communities and Vassa

Vassa is not normally practised by Mahayana Buddhists. Countries such as China and Japan do not have a rainy season in the same way as Buddhist countries further south. However, monks in these countries do take similar periods of retreat to spend time alone and meditate during the year.

Pavarana ceremony

A full moon marks the end of Vassa, usually occuring in October. On this day, monks perform a ceremony called Pavarana. They light a candle over a bowl of water and, as they chant, hot wax drips into the bowl. The water is then sprinkled on the people present to bless them.

Tavatimsa festival

In Myanmar, the Tavatimsa festival follows Vassa. Buddhists believe that the Buddha spent the months of Vassa sharing his teaching with his dead mother. They believe she was reborn in a place called the Tavatimsa heaven. Myanmar's Buddhists celebrate the Buddha's return with a festival of lights. Houses and monasteries are lit up with coloured lights. Tiny leaf boats carrying lights are released to float across rivers and lakes.

▽ Buddhists in Bangladesh light candles and hot air balloons to celebrate Pavarana.

Now & Then

Festival of Hungry Ghosts

Some Buddhist festivals are enjoyed by non-Buddhists, too. China is home to millions of Buddhists and has many distinctive festivals. The Festival of Hungry Ghosts takes place in August or September. The "hungry ghosts" of Chinese ancestors are believed to be walking around in the human world and causing trouble. Monks and nuns leave out food and chant prayers for the ghosts. Buddhists make paper boats to carry their ancestors to a better rebirth. It is a time for Buddhists and non-Buddhists to remember and honour their ancestors.

After the Rains

In the month after the end of Vassa, Theravada Buddhists celebrate Kathina. The festival marks the time when monastics can leave the place where they have stayed during Vassa. Before the festival begins, five monastics - who have all observed Vassa correctly – must be present.

Ancient origins

The festival's origins lie in the story of a group of Buddhist monks who were travelling to visit the Buddha. When the rainy season began, they were forced to stop.

The Buddha heard about this and sent them some cloth. He said that they should use the cloth to make a robe for a member of their community. The monks followed the Buddha's instructions and started to sew the new robe. They stretched the cloth on a frame, also called a kathina.

At Kathina, Buddhists offer gifts to communities of monks and nuns, particularly pieces of cloth to make new robes. The monks will decide which member of their community should receive the new robe.

Now & Then

Making robes from rags

The new robe sewn together by the monks at Kathina is made from patches of cloth. This tradition reminds Buddhists about the robes of the earliest monks, which were often made from whatever rags they could find or were given by other Buddhists. Others believe that the patches of the robe are a reminder of the rice fields that monks would see on their travels.

Merit

Buddhists try to live in a caring way, thinking about the needs and feelings of others. They believe that giving gifts at Kathina and other festivals, as well as giving daily food to monks and nuns, will bring **merit** to the giver. This will help them to improve their future rebirth.

⌃ Buddhists offering new robes to monastics in Thailand during Kathina.

PARINIRVANA DAY

Theravada Buddhists celebrate the Buddha's birth, enlightenment and death on the same day at Vesak. Mahayana Buddhists, however, celebrate these key events in the Buddha's life on other, separate days. Parinirvana Day, or **Nirvana** Day as it is sometimes called, is the day when Mahayana Buddhists remember the Buddha's final entry into nirvana at his death.

Everything changes

Parinirvana Day is not a sad time for Buddhists. They believe that the Buddha's parinirvana released him from his suffering. The idea that everything changes is at the heart of Buddhism, and is celebrated by Buddhists.

◇ This painting from South Korea celebrates the Buddha's parinirvana.

Mahayana Buddhists celebrate the festival in February. They believe that the Buddha attained parinirvana, or his final death, when he was 80 years old. Because he had already achieved enlightenment, the Buddha would not be reborn.

Buddhists believe that at this time the Buddha passed into a state of endless nirvana, or spiritual peace. Right up until his parinirvana, the Buddha continued to travel and teach those who followed him.

Time for meditation

For Buddhists, this festival is an opportunity to think about their lives. People will visit a local temple, bringing gifts and sharing a meal, but they will also find time for meditation.

Individual Buddhists think about their own progress towards Enlightenment and any changes they should make to their own lives. They also remember friends and relatives who have died recently.

⌃ Meditation is a way for Buddhists to calm and train their minds. They hope that by meditating they will gain a deeper understanding of life.

FAMILY CELEBRATIONS

Some of the most joyous Buddhist celebrations mark the different stages in a Buddhist's life. Like members of other religions, Buddhists mark life stages, particularly becoming an adult and death, with ceremonies or rites of passage. The Buddhist belief in rebirth influences these important family events.

Childhood ceremonies

There is no Buddhist ceremony when a child is born. This is unlike Christian baptism, which happens several weeks or months after a baby is born, or the Jewish Brit Milah, which takes place about eight days afterwards. Buddhist monastics may say a blessing over a newborn baby. The most important ceremony for young Buddhists is one which marks the change from childhood to adulthood.

The bride and groom bow to each other during a Buddhist-style wedding ceremony in China.

In Theravada Buddhist communities, boys will often spend time living in a monastery. Sometime between the ages of 8 and 20, their heads are shaved and they wear the orange robes of monks. Their stay in the monastery may last a few days to a few months.

At the end of this time, the boys leave the monastery as full adult members of the community, or they can choose to stay and be fully ordained as monks. Although girls can stay with communities of nuns, there is not a similar ceremony for girls as there is for boys. In any case, there has been a decline in the number of communities of nuns.

⌃ These boys are staying in a monastery in Cambodia.

Marriages

There is not one marriage service that all Buddhists follow. Marriage is seen as a social occasion rather than a religious ritual. For marriage, buddhists will follow local traditions.

In a Thai marriage ceremony, the married couple may offer food to the monks using a single spoon, so they share the merit for this. In Britain and other Western communities, where marriage is a big social celebration, Buddhist couples may arrange for a blessing before a shrine or an image of the Buddha.

⌃ Buddhists take part in a funeral procession in Vietnam.

Death and rebirth

Although Buddhists are sad when a loved one dies, they also see death as the start of a rebirth. Funerals are therefore a time to celebrate this life.

Theravada Buddhists follow the ancient Indian ritual of cremating, or burning, the body of the dead person. Ancient writings make clear that this ceremony took place when the Buddha died. Monks chant prayers as the body is being prepared for the funeral.

In Thailand, the funeral usually takes place three days after death. During this time, friends and family meet for feasts and even games. After the funeral, relatives sometimes burn the dead person's favourite possessions so that he or she can carry them into the next life. The family and friends of the dead person give gifts of food and candles to the monks and nuns. This is thought to protect the spirit before its rebirth.

Tibetan rituals

Buddhists in Tibet have very detailed beliefs about what happens to a person's spirit after death. Words from the Tibetan Book of the Dead will be read to help the dead person in the 49 days between lives.

Like many Buddhist festivals, there is an amazing variety of family ceremonies across the Buddhist world. These ceremonies and rituals are always a time for reflection on the past and look to the future.

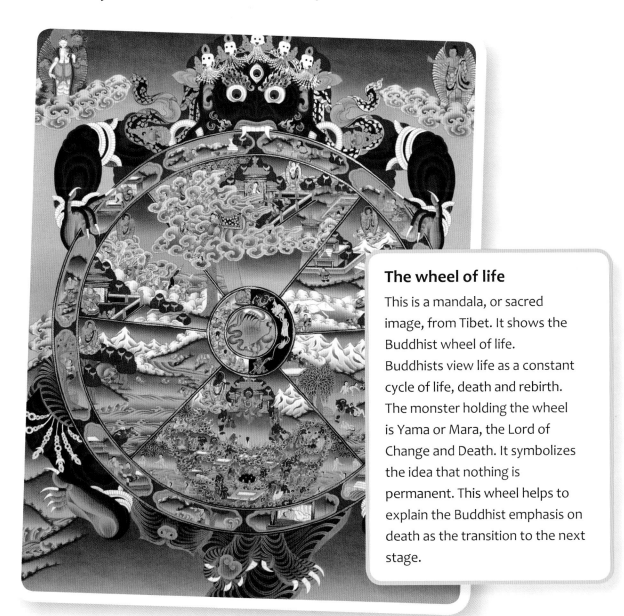

The wheel of life

This is a mandala, or sacred image, from Tibet. It shows the Buddhist wheel of life. Buddhists view life as a constant cycle of life, death and rebirth. The monster holding the wheel is Yama or Mara, the Lord of Change and Death. It symbolizes the idea that nothing is permanent. This wheel helps to explain the Buddhist emphasis on death as the transition to the next stage.

COOKERY TIPS

Vegetarian guthuk

- Traditional guthuk fortunes represent character traits, such as "lazy", "happy" or "shy". Write them on slips of paper, fold them up and roll them inside the dumplings. Place one cooked dumplings in each soup bowl right before serving. After your guests have read their fortunes, set the dumplings aside. They are not for eating.

- To knead dough, place it on a floured work surface. Fold the dough in half, and then flatten and stretch it with the heel of your hand. Repeat until the dough is smooth and stretchy.

- Sautéing is a process of cooking vegetables over high heat with a little bit of fat (such as vegetable oil). It browns the vegetables and brings out their flavours before you add other ingredients.

Potato curry

You can buy tinned diced green chilli peppers. If you use fresh ones, be careful. Chilli peppers can irritate your skin and eyes. Cut open the pepper lengthwise and remove the seeds and veins with a knife (see picture, right). Then rinse and dice it into small pieces. When you are done, wash your hands thoroughly with warm soapy water.

TIMELINE

BCE

c. 485	Siddhartha Gautama, the Buddha and founder of Buddhism, is born
405	First Buddhist Council agrees the Buddhist scriptures that could be traced back to the Buddha himself
272–231	Reign of Indian Emperor Ashoka, who sent his followers across India and beyond to teach others about Buddhism
247	Mahinda and Sanghamitta establish Buddhism in Sri Lanka, now celebrated with the Poson festival
Around 200	Beginnings of Mahayana Buddhist movements

CE

0–100	Buddhism spreads into China and Central Asia
200–300	Buddhist teachings are carried to the region that is now Thailand, Myanmar, Cambodia and Laos
300–400	Buddhism is introduced to Korea from China
552	Buddhism first enters Japan from China
600–700	Introduction of Buddhism to Tibet
633-643	Chinese monk Hsuan-Tsang visits India. He finds Buddhism in decline and many monasteries in ruins.
1907	British Buddhists form the Buddhist Society of Great Britain and Ireland

Glossary

chant form of musical verse sung by Buddhist monks and others

dharma teachings of the Buddha, and living life according to those teachings

enlightenment state of deep understanding and knowledge of life, which Buddhists believe the Buddha achieved

fast go without food or drink for a particular period of time

incense wood and plant materials that release a strong smell when burned

karma results of someone's actions, in this life or in a future life

Mahayana branch of Buddhism that is most popular in northern Asian countries, such as China and Tibet. The Mahayana branch is made up of many different groups, such as Zen Buddhism.

meditate calm or focus the mind to train it and to achieve deeper spiritual understanding

merit idea that Buddhists can gain benefit from good deeds or thoughts that they can carry with them through their lives and into their next life

monastery building where monks live

monastic monks, nuns or other members of a religious community

monk male member of the sangha who has devoted his life to understanding Buddhist teachings and helping others

nirvana state of enlightenment when a person is freed from the cycle of death and rebirth

nun female member of the sangha who has devoted her life to understanding Buddhist teachings and helping others

ordain make someone a monk or nun, through an ordination ceremony

poverty state of being very poor. If someone is in the state of poverty, they might struggle to even buy food.

privilege special right or advantage given to a certain person or group

relic ancient object that is believed to be connected to an important religious figure or event

retreat place where someone can go to meditate, relax and reflect on things

sangha Buddhist community of monks and nuns

scripture sacred writings

sermon speech on a religious subject

shrine place that is sacred because of a link to a particular holy person or object

Theravada branch of Buddhism that is most popular in Sri Lanka, Thailand, Cambodia, Laos and Myanmar

Find out more

Books
A Year of Buddhist Festivals (Festival Time), Rita Storey (Franklin Watts, 2013)
Buddhism (Special Times), Jane West (A & C Black, 2010)
Buddhism (This Is My Faith), Holly Wallace (Ticktock, 2012)

Websites
www.bbc.co.uk/religion/religions/buddhism/history/britishbuddhism_1.shtml
Find out more about the Buddhist communities in the UK.

www.bbc.co.uk/schools/religion/buddhism
On this site, there is information about Buddhism, including Buddhist festivals.

www.buddhanet.net/e-learning/basic-guide.htm
Learn more about Buddhism on this website.

Places to visit
There are many Buddhist communities in the UK and other countries. Some UK temples include:

- Buddhapadipa Temple, Wimbledon, London (**www.buddhapadipa.org**)
- Kagyu Samye Ling, Eskdalemuir, Scotland (**www.samyeling.org**)
- Manchester Buddhist Centre (**www.manchesterbuddhistcentre.org.uk**)
- Cardiff Buddhist Centre (**www.cardiffbuddhistcentre.com**)

These Buddhist communities welcome enquiries from schools. It is a good idea to contact them in advance to arrange to visit. You should always be quiet and respectful in any place of worship.

Further Reseach
- We have discovered in this book that Buddhist festivals are celebrated in different ways depending on the location. You could investigate more about Buddhism in a particular country, such as Japan or China, which can be very different from Buddhist traditions in Sri Lanka.
- Is there a Buddhist community near your home? If so, you may be able to arrange for someone to talk to you about the religion. You may be able to find out about local celebrations of Vesak or other festivals.
- There are many examples of Buddhist art, from statues to buildings. Find out more about these and the culture that has grown up around Buddhism.

INDEX